WHAT'S UP WITH WATER?

WHY DO WE NEED WATER?

by Karen Latchana Kenney

Consultant: Marla Conn, Reading Specialist, Read-Ability

BEARPORT PUBLISHING

Minneapolis, Minnesota

Teaching Tips

Before Reading

- Look at the cover of the book. Discuss the picture and the title.
- Ask readers to brainstorm a list of what they already know about why we need water. What can they expect to see in this book?
- Go on a picture walk, looking through the pictures to discuss vocabulary and make predictions about the text.

During Reading

- Read for purpose. Encourage readers to think about water and its role in life on Earth.
- Ask readers to look for the details of the story. What are the different things water does for us?
- If readers encounter an unknown word, ask them to look at the sounds in the word. Then, ask them to look at the rest of the page. Are there any clues to help them understand?

After Reading

- Encourage readers to pick a buddy and reread the book together.
- Ask readers to name three reasons from this book about why we need water. Go back and find the pages that tell about these things.
- Ask readers to write and draw a picture of something that they learned about why we need water.

Credits:
Cover, © Alter-ego/Shutterstock; Title page, © Alex Staroseltsev/Shutterstock; 3, © robert_s/Shutterstock; 5, © Robert Kneschke/Shutterstock; 6, © CK Foto/Shutterstock; 7, © atsurkan/Shutterstock; 8, © Lev Dolgachov/Alamy Stock Photo; 9, © Rido/Shutterstock; 10, © Syda Productions/Shutterstock; 11, © CK Foto/Shutterstock; 12, © lovelyday12/Shutterstock; 13, © Martin Kemp/Shutterstock and © risteski goce/Shutterstock; 14, © Hispanolistic/iStock; 15, © Lana K/Shutterstock; 16-17, © Marilyn Nieves/iStock; 18, © CK Foto/Shutterstock; 19, © Design Pics/Alamy Stock Photo; 20, © FatCamera/iStock; 21, © Yuri Samsonov/Shutterstock; 22, © Lina Truman/Shutterstock, © Lina Truman/Shutterstock, © Ron Dalev, © Pikovit/Shutterstock; 23BL, © Prostock-Studio; 23BM, © WIRACHAIPHOTO/Shutterstock; 23BR, © borgogniels/iStock; 23TL, © Robert Kneschke/Alamy Stock Photo; 23TR, © FatCamera/Getty Images

Library of Congress Cataloging-in-Publication Data is available at www.loc.gov or upon request from the publisher.

ISBN: 978-1-64747-494-2 (hardcover)
ISBN: 978-1-64747-499-7 (paperback)
ISBN: 978-1-64747-504-8 (ebook)

For more information, write to Bearport Publishing, 5357 Penn Avenue South, Minneapolis, MN 55419.

Printed in the United States of America.

Contents

Time for a Drink

On a warm day, we run and play.

The sun is hot.

Soon, we are **thirsty**!

Why do we need water?

We are made of lots of water.

What does water do?

It helps our bodies work.

It keeps us **healthy**.

Water gives us **energy**.

Tag!

You are it!

Water can help us think better.

We are ready to learn.

Drinking enough water is **important**.

It can keep us from getting sick.

It can even help us feel happy!

We need water to be our best.

So do plants and animals.

Plants need water to grow up, up, up!

Animals need water to be healthy.

How do we get water?

We can take
a big drink
from a glass
of water.

Gulp!

Water is in the
food we eat, too.

Munch, munch.

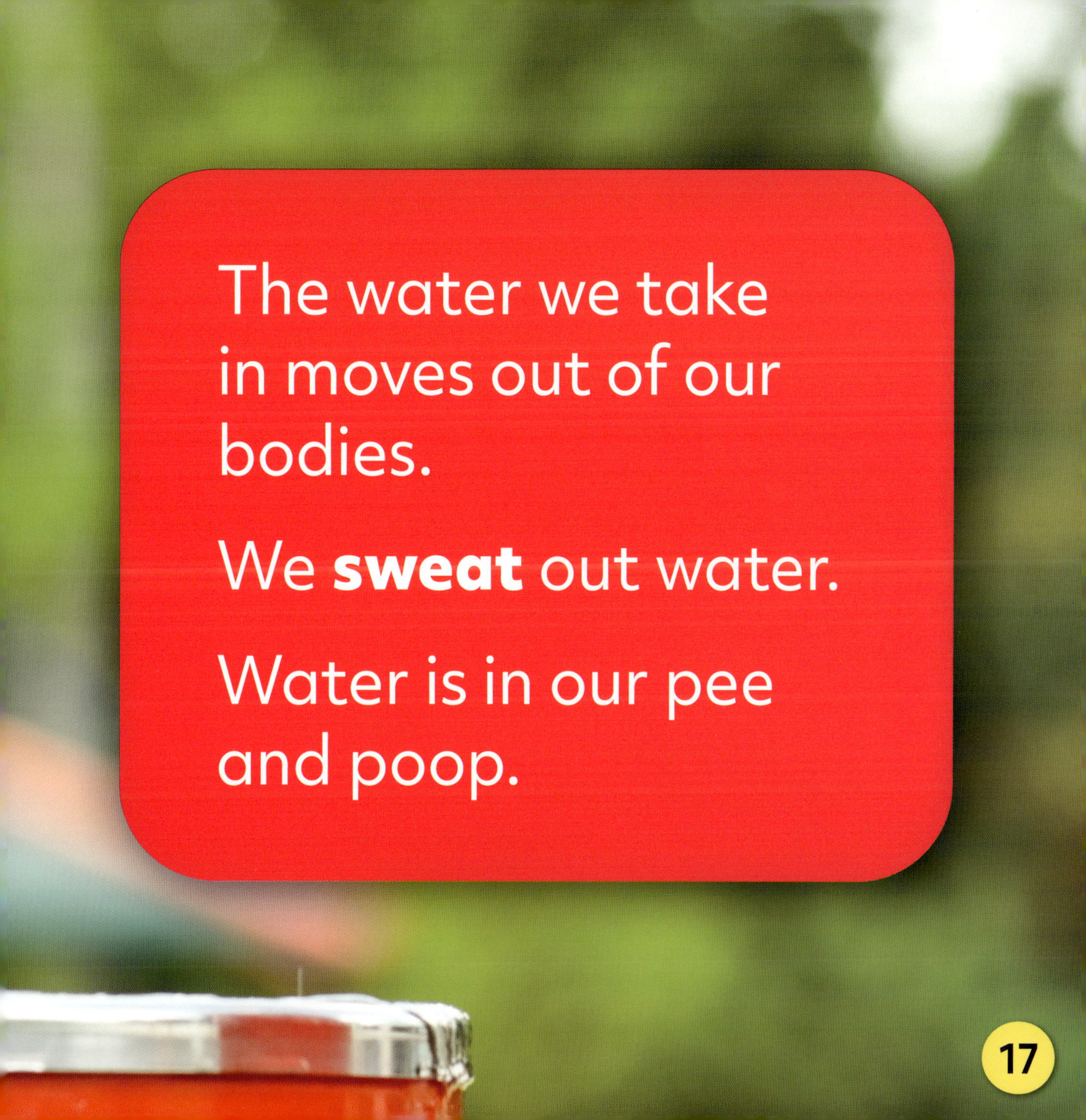

The water we take in moves out of our bodies.

We **sweat** out water.

Water is in our pee and poop.

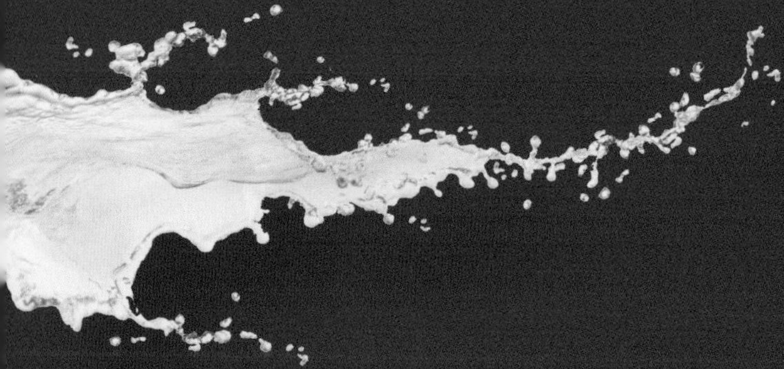

We use water in many other ways.

We wash our bodies with water.

Water helps us clean all around our homes.

We need water every day.

It keeps us strong.

It helps us stay clean and healthy.

Think of all the things water can do!

Water and Our Bodies

How does water work with our bodies?

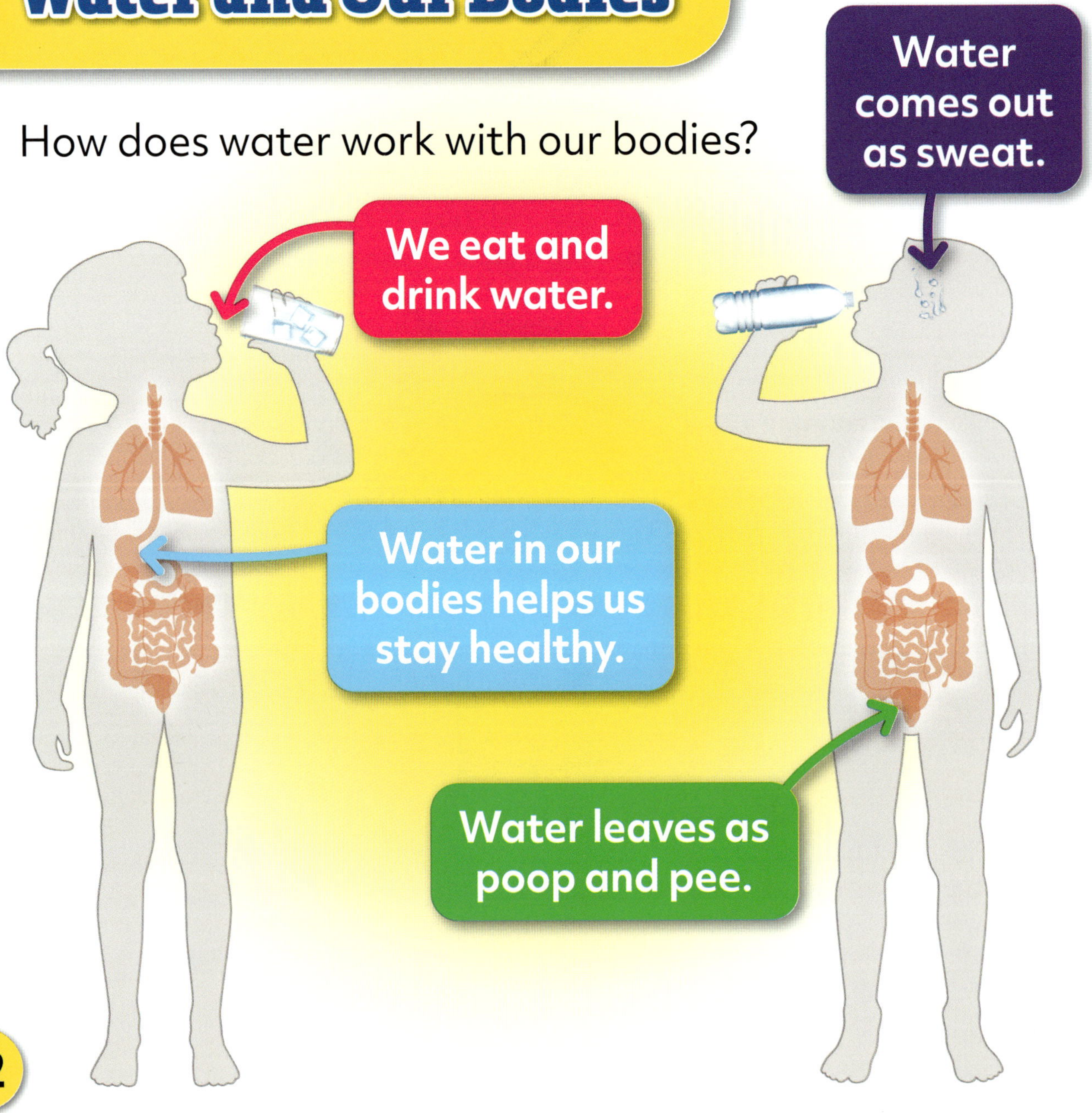

Glossary

energy power used to move, grow, and live

healthy well and not ill

important matters a lot

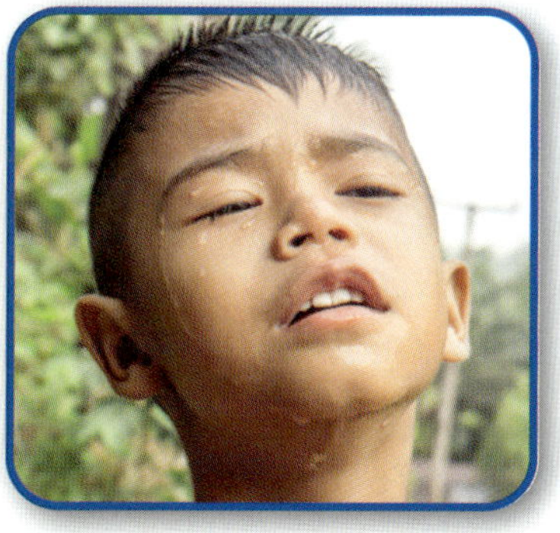

sweat water that leaves the body through the skin

thirsty feeling the need for water

Index

Read More

Aleo, Karen. *Living Things Need Water (Little Pebble. What Living Things Need).* North Mankato, MN: Pebble, 2020.

Lindeen, Mary. *What Plants Need (A Beginning to Read Book).* Chicago: Norwood House Press, 2019.

Learn More Online

1. Go to **www.factsurfer.com**
2. Enter "**Need Water**" into the search box.
3. Click on the cover of this book to see a list of websites.

About the Author

Karen Latchana Kenney writes and edits books about water, nature, and famous scientists. She lives in Minnesota with her husband and son.